At the End of Time

by Derek Prince

BOOKS BY DEREK PRINCE

At the End of Time

by Derek Prince

AT THE END OF TIME

© 2010 Derek Prince Ministries–International

This edition DPM-UK 2012
All rights reserved.

Published by DPM-UK
Kingsfield, Hadrian Way,
Baldock, SG7 6AN, UK
www.dpmuk.org

ISBN 978-1-908594-23-5

Product Code: B107

Derek Prince Ministries
www.derekprince.com

AT THE END OF TIME

This booklet is part of a series based on the six foundation doctrines of Hebrews 6:1–2, which follow:

- Repentance from dead works
- Faith toward God
- The doctrine of baptisms
- Laying on of hands
- Resurrection of the dead
- Eternal judgment

Thus far in our studies, we have dealt with the first four doctrines which are within our present Christian experience. However, the two doctrines that remain move us out of the present and into eternity: "the resurrection of the dead" and "eternal judgment." The study of these two truths should challenge and excite our hearts as we consider what awaits us in the future. By way of introduction to these doctrines, we will explore a theme in this booklet entitled *At the End of Time*.

As we approach the final two doctrines, we are being taken out of time and focused on eternity. One of the important functions of these last two doctrines is to teach us that we should not focus on this life only. Many Christians today think only in terms of what God will do for them in this life. However, this life is just a tiny fraction of all that God has for us.

Brought Out of Time

We begin with a Scripture from Revelation 10 which speaks about an angel:

> *The angel which I saw stand upon the sea and upon the earth lifted up his hand to heaven, and sware by him [God] that liveth for ever and ever, who created heaven, and the things that therein are, and the earth, and the things that therein are, and the sea, and the things which are therein, that there should be time no longer: but in the days of the voice of the seventh angel, when he shall begin to sound, the mystery of God should be finished, as he hath declared to his servants the prophets.*
>
> *Revelation 10:5–7 KJV*

Almost all translations of the Bible say at the end of verse 6, "there will be no more delay," which may be the correct meaning. But what the Scripture actually says is "there shall be no more time." With my background in philosophy, I find this concept most compelling. We are coming to a point in every one of our lives when, sooner or later, there will be no more time. Somebody has said, "The clock behind all clocks is the human heart, and when the human heart ceases to beat, all clocks cease to tick." Each of us will individually pass out of time into a new, eternal realm.

Eternity is not just a very long period of time. It is a totally different realm of being, one that we can scarcely comprehend.

Time Is a Mystery

I appreciate the statement, "the mystery of God should be finished" (Revelation 10:7), because time is a mystery.

I was deeply involved with the topic of time as a philosopher more than fifty years ago. But this subject appeals to me now because the Bible says so clearly that time is part of the mystery which is now finished at this point in Revelation. Physicists tell us that if someone could board a spaceship that travels at near the

8

speed of light, visit a distant star and come back, by the traveler's time, that person would have been maybe two years on the journey. But by earth's time, it would have been two generations. When that person came back, he would meet his great-grandchildren! That boggles our minds. Time is a mystery.

The measurement of time, as we understand it, depends on a human observer. For instance, scientists might tell us that based on the accumulation of the deposit of sediment in a certain valley they believe that one million years have passed.

I could say that I believe that, too. But I believe it happened one million times faster than they say it did and only one year had really passed. There would be no difference whatever in the evidence.

In other words, it is the input of a personal observer that makes time what it is. I am content to say it is a mystery. Bear in mind, however, that one day we are going to pass out of time into eternity.

Eternal or Temporary?

Second Corinthians 4:17–18 speaks about the difference between the eternal and the temporary. Paul says:

> *For our light affliction, which is but for a moment, is working for us a far more exceeding and eternal weight of glory . . .*   *2 Corinthians 4:17*

Considering all that Paul suffered, when he speaks about a "light affliction," I wonder what we are worrying about! What are we going through that compares to what Paul experienced? We can't talk about deep afflictions until we have measured ourselves by Paul.

Always bear in mind that when we are under pressure it is doing something for us. Pressure is working to produce in us a far more exceeding and eternal weight of glory. In the Hebrew language, the word for "weight" and the word for "glory" are essentially the same. So Paul, thinking in Hebrew, is speaking about a weight of glory that God is preparing for us. Then he continues:

*. . . while we do not look at the things which
are seen, but at the things which are not seen.*
verse 18

We need to understand that affliction only works good in our
lives while we keep our eyes on the eternal. If we take our eyes
off the eternal and instead start to focus on our problems and feel
sorry for ourselves, our affliction is not doing us any good. It only
works for us:

*. . . while we do not look at the things which are seen, but
at the things which are not seen. For the things which are
seen are temporary, but the things which are not seen are
eternal.*
verse 18

Here Paul is putting before us two different realms: the realm
of what is visible (physical, material, and temporary) and the realm
of what is invisible (spiritual and eternal). Remember, everything
that we encounter in this life in the stream of time is temporary.

Where Are We Headed?

It is very important to bear in mind that we are headed for a
realm that is eternal. I once read in a little devotional book a very
simple statement: "We live in a fallen world." That is so true. If
we are objectively honest, we must admit that in the world as we
know it there is much more misery than happiness. There is much
more strife than peace. There is much more sickness than health.

We can't paint a pretty picture of the world, because we live
in a fallen world that has been thoroughly marred, corrupted, and
tainted by sin. Thank God, our final destiny is not in this world
as we know it!

Paul makes a statement in 1 Corinthians 15:9 that deeply
impacts me: "If in this life only we have hope in Christ, we are
of all men the most pitiable [to be pitied]." Ponder this statement
for a moment. If all we expect from Christ is in this life only, we

are the most pitiable. Yet, I meet so many Christians who seem to be totally preoccupied with what happens in this life. Their concept of Christianity is getting something from God in this world. This preoccupation is absolutely alien to the teaching of the New Testament.

What Do We Seek?

It is very healthy for us to be pressured by the Holy Spirit into considering the end of time and the beginning of eternity in our lives. In Hebrews 13:14 the writer says:

For here we have no continuing city, but we seek [look for] *the one to come.*

Is that true of each of us? Where is our permanence in life? Is it in this world only, or do we realize that this life is only temporary? As the spiritual song says, "We are just passing through." Our permanent destination is in eternity.

If we can only see the things of this present life, we will be unhappy, frustrated individuals, always complaining, "Things aren't going the way I want. God isn't answering my prayers."

The source of our discontent is choosing a temporal perspective rather than viewing everything in the perspective of eternity. Therefore, we need to ask how much we are building into our lives for eternity. I have come to the conclusion that God will not sacrifice the tiniest portion of eternity for the greatest length of time, because time is not permanent. Eternity is.

Enduring Riches

Scripture says in Proverbs that God has given us, through wisdom, enduring riches (see Proverbs 8:18). I have spent a lot of time pondering this question: What are enduring riches?

Riches that endure are not money in the bank, stocks and shares, the fancy cars we drive, the homes we live in or the swimming pools in our backyards. None of those are enduring riches. What,

11

then, are enduring riches? Jesus said:

> *"Sell what you have and give to the poor, and you will have treasure in heaven."*   Matthew 19:21

"Treasure in heaven" is enduring riches. Jesus also said that whatever you give to the cause of the gospel, God will give it back a hundredfold in eternity. (See Matthew 19:29.) That is a ten thousand percent increase. How many businessmen would turn down the opportunity to gain a ten thousand percent return on an investment?

Godly character is also eternal wealth. All our spiritual gifts—our prophecy, our miracles, our words of knowledge—will cease when life ends. We will not take them with us. They are only for this world and the realm of time. But we will take our character into eternity. Character is permanent, and our character will determine what we will be throughout eternity. For us to build pure, strong, godly, Christian character is to build lasting, enduring riches.

Biblical Prophecy

As we approach a study of eternal matters, we need a basic understanding of biblical prophecy. Unfortunately, many people have lost confidence in biblical prophecy because of false, flashy, and shallow interpretations of Scripture. However, never let the misuse of something good turn you away from what is good.

In my lifetime, I have seen all the gifts of the Spirit misused at one time or another. But that has not caused me to despise the gifts of the Spirit. It just makes me more careful as to how I use them.

The same is true of biblical prophecy. We need it, because without it, we are stumbling in the dark. We simply need to be careful how we apply it.

> *And so we have the prophetic word made more sure, to which you do well to pay attention* [heed] *as to a lamp shining in a dark place, until the day dawns and the morning star arises in your hearts. But know this first of*

all, that no prophecy of Scripture is a matter of one's own
interpretation, for no prophecy was ever made by an act
of human will, but men moved by the Holy Spirit spoke
from God.   *2 Peter 1:19–21*

The "prophetic word" is the written prophecies of the Bible. We are not referring to the gift of prophesying, although that has its place in our lives. This is the written prophecies of the Bible, "to which you do well to pay attention [heed] as to a lamp shining in a dark place."

We cannot afford to despise the prophetic Scriptures, because Peter says they are a lamp shining in a dark place. The world in which we live today is undoubtedly a dark place. Furthermore, it is getting darker. We need a light that will guide us through the darkness. And the light God has provided is the prophetic revelation of Scripture.

It is possible to be wonderfully saved and a good Christian but still walk in the dark because we have not availed ourselves of the light of prophetic Scripture. When we walk in the dark we will stumble over objects we need not run into. Without a clear understanding of the prophetic word, we really do not know where we are going or understand what is happening in the world around us. Therefore, especially in these days, the prophetic word is extremely important.

Peter goes on to say that we need to give heed to it "until the day dawns and the morning star arises in your hearts" (2 Peter 1:19 NASB). This is not referring to the coming of Jesus. Rather, this is an inner, subjective, personal experience as the morning star shines in our hearts. In the natural realm, the morning star immediately precedes the rise of the sun. Do you know what the morning star in our hearts does? It tells us Jesus is coming back, which gives us hope in the midst of darkness and a sense of excitement about the future.

If you have never been excited about the return of the Lord, that event has apparently not meant much to you. Jesus' return is the only hope for humanity. Nothing else can ever meet all the desperate needs of the human race.

When people talk about His return as "pie in the sky," don't believe it! The return of the Lord is totally realistic. In fact, I think it is unrealistic to expect a merely human solution to the problems of humanity.

I believe it is utterly unrealistic, for instance, to expect politicians to solve the problems of humanity. They have been trying a long time and it seems the mess only gets worse.

Human solutions to the world's problems is the teaching of Humanism, which is an anti-Christian force at work in world governments today. We need prophecy today more than ever because, as Peter goes on to say, it does not originate with men, but it comes from God.

Two Keys

There are two keys to understanding biblical prophecy. In Deuteronomy 29:29 Moses said to the children of Israel:

"The secret things belong to the LORD our God, but those things which are revealed belong to us and to our children forever, that we may do all the words of this law."

Moses said there are two kinds of things—the secret things and the things that are revealed. The secret things belong to God and nobody can understand them. The things that are revealed are for us to act on. The main reason people get off track in their study of prophecy is that they try to understand the secret things (which belong to God) while at the same time not obey the things that are revealed (which belong to us).

Whenever I speak on prophecy, somebody almost always asks, "Are you pre-, mid-, or post-?" They mean "pre-tribulation," "mid-tribulation," or "post-tribulation." I always answer, "I don't know!" I am not ashamed that I don't know. Furthermore, I don't believe anybody knows. Even Jesus does not know, because Scripture says the day and the hour of His return no one knows, not even the Son, only the Father. (See Matthew 24:36 and Mark 13:32.)

14

So, if I don't know something that Jesus doesn't know, I am not embarrassed by it.

Confusion comes when people want to know things that cannot be known. The motivation behind that is pride, which is the most dangerous of all motivations. If we have revealed truth and obey it, God will give us more. If we do not obey it, He will not give us more.

You may say, "God, please show me what comes next." But He might well reply, "You haven't acted on what I've already shown you. Why should I show you any more?"

The first key to the effective use of biblical prophecy is knowing the things God wants us to understand and not bothering Him about the things that He does not want us to understand.

The second key is, whatever God reveals to you, act on it and obey it. In my opinion, one clear revelation of biblical prophecy is contained in Matthew 24:14:

"This gospel of the kingdom will be preached in all the world as a witness to all the nations, and then the end will come."

When will the end come? When this gospel of the kingdom has been preached in all the world as a witness to all the nations. Whose job is that? Ours. If we are not working on obeying that revelation, why should God tell us any more? However, if we will begin to work on that revelation and begin to devote ourselves in whatever way is appropriate to getting the gospel of the kingdom out to all nations, we will be surprised at what God will show us next.

If we have not acted on the revealed things, why should He show us any more?

End-Time Events

As a picture of the close of this age, we will consider certain general statements about the kinds of events that will be going on as this age comes to a close. I believe we live near the close of the age—that is my personal opinion. I would not want to set dates, but I could believe that within the next fifty years everything that is written in the Book could have happened. I am not saying it *will* happen, but I could believe it *could.*

As the age comes to a close, righteousness and wickedness will both increase. Righteousness will flourish, and so will wickedness. Light will shine, and there will be great darkness. We must get adjusted to this antithesis between these two aspects of light and darkness, righteousness and wickedness.

As we consider certain features of the close of the age, there are three especially significant Scriptures.

The first is Isaiah 60 where the Lord is speaking to His people. He says:

> *Arise, shine; for your light has come! And the glory of the LORD is risen upon you. For behold, the darkness shall cover the earth, and deep darkness the peoples; but the LORD will arise over you, and His glory will be seen upon you. The Gentiles* [nations] *shall come to your light, and kings to the brightness of your rising.*
> *Isaiah 60:1–3*

This is a promise for God's people at the close of the age. The glory of God will shine upon us and in the midst of the dense darkness that is surrounding us on all sides, covering all nations. Then those who have a heart for truth will come out of the darkness to the people of God to seek the light. Do not expect the darkness to end. It will continue, and it will grow deeper. But correspondingly, the light will get brighter.

There is a wonderful fact about light and darkness that goes back to the creation. Wherever light meets darkness, it is light that wins. Just bear in mind that if we are the light and we are in the light, we win.

The second significant passage is the parable of the wheat and the tares found in Matthew 13:24–30. This parable is about a farmer who sowed good seed in his field. Then, in the night an enemy came and sowed tares (weeds), which apparently looked like wheat. But there was just one major difference: the tares had no fruit. The tares did not produce anything worth having.

The workers in the field said, "Shall we go and pull up the tares?" The farmer said, "No, because when you try to pull up the tares you'll pull up some of the wheat. Let them both grow together to harvest."

In interpreting His parable, Jesus said, "The harvest is the end of the age" (verse 30). He tells us that at the end of the age the angels will come forth and sever the wicked from among the righteous. The wicked will be bound up in bundles and cast into the fire, and the righteous will shine as sons in the kingdom of their Father.

Bear in mind that right up to the close of the age, the wheat and the tares will be growing up side by side. The church is not going to be fully purified until the end of the age. Even then we are not going to be separating the wheat from the tares. The angels are going to do that.

This parable is not speaking about the pagan world, but about professing Christendom. In that situation, both wheat and tares will grow side by side. If you want to be sure you are wheat and not tares, check on the fruit that you are producing, because that is the difference.

The third passage for consideration is in Revelation 22, near the end of the Bible, where we find a statement first from an angel of God, and then a statement from Jesus Himself:

He [the angel that brought the revelation] said to me, "Do not seal the words of the prophecy of this book, for the time is at hand. He who is unjust [unrighteous]*, let him be unjust* [unrighteous] *still; he who is filthy, let him be filthy still; he who is righteous, let him be righteous still; he who is holy, let him be holy still."*
                                                    Revelation 22:10–11

This is a remarkable statement coming from God and delivered by an angel. He says, in effect, "If you want to be unrighteous, go on. You don't have long, so live it up. If you want to be filthy, be still more filthy. But if you are righteous, be still more righteous.

If you are holy, be still more holy, because this is the parting of the ways."

In the next verse, Jesus Himself is speaking and He says:

"Behold, I am coming quickly, and My reward is with Me, to give to every one according to his work."
verse 12

This declaration is spoken immediately before the return of the Lord. The wicked and the righteous are side by side—the wicked getting more wicked, the righteous getting more righteous.

In the spiritual realm, we cannot remain static. We are either going forward or backward. Proverbs says, "The path of the righteous is like the light of dawn, that shines brighter and brighter until the full day" (Proverbs 4:38 NASB). Righteousness is not stationary; rather, it is a pathway we must move along.

If we are moving in the path of righteousness, the light is getting brighter every day. But if we are living today by yesterday's light, we are beginning to be a backslider and we are not continuing in the pathway of righteousness.

How to Respond

In the midst of prophecies about dark times, Jesus offers us some beautiful words of comfort in Luke 21:25–28, speaking about the close of the age:

"There will be signs in the sun, in the moon, and in the stars; and on the earth distress of nations, with perplexity, the sea and the waves roaring; men's hearts failing them from fear and the expectation of those things which are coming on the earth, for the powers of the heavens will be shaken. Then they will see the Son of Man coming in a cloud with power and great glory. [Jesus is speaking to His disciples:] Now when these things begin to happen, look up and lift up your heads, because your redemption draws near."

Jesus said the whole globe is going to be shaken. How do you react to all the promises of turmoil and the conflict? Do you get depressed and discouraged? Or do you say, "Praise God, our redemption is very near"? Your reaction tells you where your heart is.

In Matthew 24, Jesus spoke about the traumatic birth pangs of a new age. I have never given birth to a baby, of course, but I understand it is not an easy experience. Birth pangs are associated with giving birth. The question for the mother is, "Do you want the baby?" If she wants the baby, she will put up with the birth pangs. However, without birth pangs, there will be no baby.

Our attitude of heart is revealed by our response to the birth pangs. If we say, when things are getting worse and worse, "Oh, this is so depressing! I feel so miserable. Where is God? I don't see Him doing anything," then we are rejecting the birth pangs. Really, it means that we are not waiting for the baby.

The baby in this case is the birth of the kingdom of God on earth. The kingdom of God will not come without birth pangs—they are guaranteed. What we must determine is how we will respond when they come.

In the midst of the increasing darkness and birth pangs, the church has a task to complete: Proclaiming the gospel of the kingdom to all nations.

The birth pangs are pictured in Matthew 24, beginning at verse 7:

> *"For nation will rise against nation* [ethnos against ethnos—ethnic conflicts] *and kingdom against kingdom. And there will be famines, pestilences, and earthquakes in various places. All these are the beginning of sorrows* [birth pangs]. *"*   *verses 7–8*

If we want the baby we must endure the birth pangs. There is no alternative.

Increasing Pressures

There follows this section on birth pangs a series of *then*s, as Jesus continues:

> *"**Then** they will deliver you up to tribulation and kill you, and you will be hated by all nations for My name's sake."*
>
> *verse 9*

Who is the *you* referred to here? "You" is "us." That may not be good grammar, but it is the truth. "They will deliver *you*"—you and me—Christians. We will be hated by all nations for the sake of Jesus' name.

> *"And **then** many will be offended, will betray one another, and will hate one another."*
>
> *verse 10*

The *many* is "many Christians." The pressure will be too great and they will give up their faith, betraying their fellow believers to save their own skins. Pressure of this kind has been happening in Communist and Islamic countries for a generation or two and it will come to the rest of the world.

> *"**Then** many false prophets will rise up and deceive many."*
>
> *verse 11*

The world is full of false prophets, many of whom are inside the church. That may come as a complete surprise to many people, but it is a subject we must leave for another study.

> *"And because lawlessness will abound, the love of many will grow cold."*
>
> *verse 12*

Do we see lawlessness increasing in the world today? I don't think anybody would say no. Jesus said lawlessness would abound, with the result that the love of many Christians would grow cold. The word for "love" there is *agape*, the word used specifically for Christian love. Under the pressure of the lawlessness in the world, some of us will let our love grow cold.

Enduring to the End

The next verse is very significant:

"But he who endures to the end shall be saved."
verse 13

The Greek is more specific, it says, "He who has endured to the end shall be saved." How do you stay saved? You have to endure. You are saved now, but to remain saved you must endure. I tell people (and nobody really blesses me for saying this): There is only one way to learn to endure and that is by enduring! If you are in the midst of enduring right now, bear in mind God is training you to live it through—to endure—to the end of the age.

Then the next verse says:

"And this gospel of the kingdom will be preached in all the world as a witness to all the nations, and then the end will come." *verse 14*

You may say, "Well, when times get easier, we'll go out and preach the gospel." No, no! Times are going to get harder and harder. It is going to take guts to go out and preach the gospel. "Guts" is a rather vulgar American word which, simply translated, means "intestinal fortitude." We need Christians with guts.

The situation is not going to get any easier; it is going to get harder. If you think it is too hard now, how will you do if it gets any harder? Jesus wants a Church that is not going to be deterred by opposition or persecution but is committed to Him, His purposes and His tasks.

Events after the Return of Jesus

We now consider events that are associated with the return of Jesus. This list will not necessarily be in the correct order because I don't really know what the correct order should be. I have met some Bible scholars who believe they know the correct order. The trouble is, they do not agree with one another, so they could not all be right. I am prepared to leave the order of events with the Lord, because I have made it my practice not to badger God for answers.

David said, "Surely I have calmed and quieted my soul, like a weaned child with his mother; like a weaned child is my soul within me. O Israel, hope in the LORD" (Psalm 131:2).

Years ago I preached regularly to large audiences of Africans. The front two rows would be occupied by nursing mothers and whenever a baby started to cry, the mother would begin to nurse the child. I noticed that an unweaned child just makes a fuss when it wants food, but a weaned child waits for the mother to prepare the food.

David said, in effect, "My soul is like a weaned child, content to wait. I don't badger God with my problems and questions; I allow Him to show me the things He wants to show me."

The key to understanding biblical prophecy is to let the Holy Spirit focus your attention on the things He wants to show you at any given time rather than fussing impatiently like an unweaned child.

The resurrection of true Christians

The first event associated with the return of Jesus is the rapture. Some Christian scholars will tell you the word *rapture* is not found in the New Testament, which is rather a naive statement, because it depends on what translation you use. As we will shortly understand, any translation that contains the word *rapture* would be perfectly accurate. The Lord says, through the apostle Paul:

> *For this we say to you by the word of the Lord, that we who are alive and remain until the coming of the Lord will by no means precede those who are asleep.*
> *1 Thessalonians 4:15*

Paul refers here to those who have died. He states that simply because we are alive when the Lord comes will not mean we will meet the Lord sooner than the ones who have died. On the contrary, Paul says:

22

For the Lord Himself will descend from heaven with a
shout, with the voice of an archangel, and with the trumpet
of God. verse 16

Some believe in a secret rapture. To me, however, there is nothing that could be more public than an event which is announced from heaven with a shout, the voice of an archangel, and the trumpet of God. How much secrecy is left at the end of that?

And the dead in Christ will rise first. [Before we who are alive are changed.] *Then we who are alive and remain shall be caught up together with them in the clouds to meet the Lord in the air. And thus we shall always be with the Lord.*
verses 16–17

The words "caught up" could perfectly well be translated "raptured." The word *rapture* comes from a Latin word which means "to seize something forcibly." In Greek, it is used of a thief entering a house and stealing something. It is used of a wolf coming among sheep and taking a sheep from the flock. It basically indicates a sudden, forceful grab.

That is what the rapture will be like. Jesus will grab us; He will reach down and take us suddenly, forcefully. There is just one difference between Jesus and the thief. The thief takes what does not belong to him; Jesus will take only those who belong to Him, "those who are Christ's at His coming" (1 Corinthians 15:23).

Paul says, "We who are alive and remain shall be caught up." He says elsewhere that we will be changed in a moment, in the blink of an eye (1 Corinthians 15:52). This is very exciting to me.

Imagine that you are sitting in a meeting, looking at a fellow Christian. He is looking at you and he blinks. Suddenly you are totally changed; you are a glorious, shining creature. He is changed, too. You look at him in amazement! It doesn't take a long time. In a moment, the twinkling of an eye, we shall be totally transformed.

Do you believe God can do that? I do, and it is exciting.

The judgment of Christians

Some Christians do not realize it, but we will be the first to be judged. Peter said judgment must "begin at the house of God" (1 Peter 4:17). The "house of God" is the church.

For we [Christians] *must all appear before the judgment seat of Christ . . .*   *2 Corinthians 5:10*

The word translated "appear" means actually "to be made manifest." It is a very frightening word. Everything about us will be totally known. There will be no secrets. All will be made manifest before the judgment seat of Christ.

The word for "judgment seat" is the Greek word *bema*. It is what a Roman official sat on when he conducted judgment. Pontius Pilate sat on a *bema* when he judged Jesus.

There will be a different judgment—a great white throne—for the judgment of all mankind at the very end. But "the judgment seat of Christ" is for Christians. But please remember that "there is therefore now no condemnation to those who are in Christ Jesus" (Romans 8:1).

The judgment seat of Christ is not a judgment of condemnation. It is a judgment to assess the quality of our service and to give the appropriate rewards. Paul says we must all appear before the judgment seat of Christ:

. . . that each one may receive the things done in the body, according to what he has done, whether good or bad.
2 Corinthians 5:10

Notice, there are only two categories: good or bad. John says in his first epistle: "All unrighteousness is sin" (1 John 5:17). Anything that is not righteous is sinful.

Allow me to give an example. If somebody asked me to illustrate the word *crooked*, I would show them a straight line and say, "Anything that deviates from this line is crooked." It may deviate by one degree or it may deviate by ninety degrees.

But it is still crooked.

This is the principle John is applying to righteousness. Anything that is unrighteous is sinful. Anything that is not good is bad. There is no middle ground.

This is a deception the enemy has foisted upon the church. "You are not doing what's right, but you are not really doing what's bad either." According to the Scripture, that is not possible. It is either one or the other.

Christ's overthrow of the Antichrist and his forces

In his first epistle, John speaks about antichrist in three ways: "the spirit of antichrist," "many antichrists," and "the Antichrist" (1 John 4:3; 2:18).

"The spirit of antichrist" is the spirit that operates through every antichrist.

The "many antichrists" have been in the world since the second century A.D. One of the most significant was Bar Kochba who claimed to be the messiah and led the Jewish people in the final revolt against Rome. The rebellion was utterly suppressed and the whole nation was either killed or taken into captivity.

Another antichrist was Sabbatai Zevi in the 17th century who claimed to be the messiah, promising to take the Jewish people back to the Middle East and plant them in their land. He went to the Middle East, was arrested by the Turks and converted to Islam.

The Jewish encyclopedia records about forty false messiahs that have come to the Jewish people since the time of Jesus. Jesus said, "Many will come in My name, saying, 'I am the Christ [Messiah],' and will deceive many" (Matthew 24:5). So there have been many antichrists, both inside and outside of the church.

But "the Antichrist" has not yet come. I personally believe his shadow has fallen across the stage of human history, but he has not yet emerged. The final Antichrist will be the embodiment of all that is evil and satanic. When he rules humanity, which he will for about three and a half years, it will be the worst period in human history. God will permit this because He says to the human race, "You've made your choice; see what you've chosen.

You have rejected Me. You have rejected My Son. This is the alternative. Help yourself."

Have you discovered that God doesn't teach just in theory? You may think, "I really learned that principle!" But God says, "Now let's see it worked out in your life!" That is going to be true of all humanity, too. The reign of the Antichrist will be the most terrible lesson the human race has ever had.

Pontius Pilate brought two men before the Jewish people: Jesus and Barabbas. Barabbas was a criminal, a violent man and an agitator. Pilate said, "Which of these do you want me to release?" The Jews said, "Give us Barabbas and crucify Jesus." (See Matthew 27:11–26). As a result, the Jewish people got Barabbas.

Then they said to Pilate, "We have no king but Caesar," which was an amazing thing for Jewish people to say! As a result of those two choices, the Jews have been ruled by the Caesars for the next nineteen centuries, and the Barabbases have been turned loose on them. This simple sentence really is the essence of Jewish history.

At the end of this age the human race will do something similar. Mankind will say, "We don't want this Christ. Give us the leader of our choice. This brilliant, talented, supernaturally empowered man—we want him." What happened with the Jews is going to happen to the human race. We are going to get what we choose. Those of us who choose Jesus will be under His government. Those of us who reject Jesus will be under the government of the Antichrist.

The overthrow of the Antichrist is depicted in Revelation 19 where Jesus appears from heaven riding on a white horse. (Do you believe there are horses in heaven?)

He who sat on him was called Faithful and True, and in righteousness He judges and makes war. [Notice, Jesus makes war.] *His eyes were like a flame of fire, and on His head were many crowns* [diadems]. *Now out of His mouth goes a sharp sword, that with it He should strike the nations. And He Himself will rule them* [the nations] *with a rod of iron. He Himself treads the winepress of the fierceness and wrath of Almighty God. And He has on His*

robe and on His thigh a name written: King of kings and
Lord of lords.   *Revelation 19:11–16*

This is Jesus coming forth as God's appointed ruler to deal with the wicked. It is quite interesting that the final book of the Bible, Revelation, has two characters that are set in opposition to one another. One is the Lamb, the other is the beast. The Lamb is Jesus, the beast is the Antichrist.

The word "the Lamb" occurs twenty-eight times in the book of Revelation. "The beast" occurs thirty-three times in reference to the Antichrist. This is the end-time conflict—between the beast and the Lamb—and the Lamb wins! That is a lesson for us, because we do not win by violence; we do not win by hatred; and we do not win by being tough. We win by laying our lives down like Jesus.

In Revelation 5, John is weeping because no one was there to open the scroll. One of the elders said, "Don't weep; it's all right. The Lion of the tribe of Judah has prevailed" (Revelation 5:5). Jesus still is the Lion of the tribe of Judah.

Judah is the name from which we get the word *Jew.* Jesus is still a Jew. He did not become a Jew just for thirty-three years—He identified with the tribe of Judah for time and for eternity. Bear in mind that when you get mixed up with the Jews, you are getting mixed up with the brothers and sisters of Jesus, so you had better be careful!

And I saw the beast, and the kings of the earth, and their armies, gathered together to make war against Him who sat on the horse and against His army. Then the beast was captured, and with him the false prophet who worked signs in his presence, by which he deceived those who received the mark of the beast and those who worshiped his image. These two were cast alive into the lake of fire burning with brimstone. And the rest [of their followers] *were killed with the sword which proceeded from the mouth of Him who sat on the horse. And all the birds were filled with their flesh.*   *Revelation 19:19–21*

The birds are God's garbage collection system. They will clean up everything, and all they will leave is clean bones. This is the final destiny of the Antichrist and all who choose to follow him—they are left as garbage on the face of the earth for the carrion birds to devour.

Salvation and restoration of Israel

In the midst of all this darkness and tribulation, Israel—the Jewish people who have been displaced from the center of history for nineteen centuries—are coming back into the center of history.

Israel today is a very small land, smaller than Wales, smaller even than the state of New Hampshire. Its population is only about seven million Jews and about one and a half million non-Jews. Yet despite its small size, Israel is in the news almost every day. Scarcely a day passes without a report from Israel, because Israel is coming back into center stage for the climax of the age and because the Jews must be in the land of Israel when the climax comes.

Romans 11 contains a very important revelation. These words are addressed by Paul to Christians from a Gentile background; that is, non-Jews.

> *For I do not desire, brethren, that you should be ignorant of this mystery* [this secret that God has been keeping], *lest you should be wise in your own opinion, that blindness* [hardening] *in part has happened to Israel until the fullness* [full number] *of the Gentiles has come in. And so all Israel will be saved.   Romans 11:25–26*

Paul addresses us as Gentiles telling us that we should not get conceited, thinking of ourselves more highly than we ought to think. (See Romans 12:3.)

The mystery is that hardening in part has happened to Israel. Notice that it is hardening in part. The whole of the Jewish people has never been totally hardened. There have always been Jews in every generation who believed in Jesus even though they were often a very small minority.

This hardening in part has happened to Israel not forever, but

28

until. The hardening is until the full number of the Gentiles has come in, until the church has done its job and proclaimed "this gospel of the kingdom" to all nations.

Meanwhile, the Lord has begun to gather in the Gentile harvest. I believe the greatest harvest the Church has ever seen is still ahead of us and that millions of people are going to come into the kingdom of God. But all this will be preparatory to the restoration of Israel.

Then Paul continues in verse 26: "And so all Israel will be saved." Israel is the only nation of which the Bible predicts that all the nation will be saved. It does not say "all New Zealand," "all Britain," or "all America"—but "all Israel" will be saved.

On the other hand, the "all Israel" to which Paul is referring is not all the Israel which is alive now, for in Romans 9:27 Paul quotes Isaiah, saying:

Though the number of the children of Israel be as the sand of the sea, the remnant will be saved.

"The remnant" is the remnant God has foreknown and chosen for Himself out of the Jewish people. Thus, the "all Israel" who will be saved is not all the Jewish people that are presently alive in the land of Israel. It is the remnant that God will bring through great tribulation, testing and suffering to make them His.

Judgment of the Gentile nations

Once Israel has been restored, Jesus will judge the Gentile nations, as pictured by the prophet Joel. This is very important for us who are not Jewish to understand. Here God is speaking through the prophet:

"For behold, in those days and at that time when I bring back the captives [exiles] *of Judah and Jerusalem . . ."*
Joel 3:1

"Those days" are the days in which we are living when God is bringing back Jewish exiles from more than one hundred nations to their own land. God says:

> *"I will also gather all* [Gentile] *nations and bring them down to the Valley of Jehoshaphat* [Jehoshaphat in Hebrew means "the Lord judges"] *and I will enter into judgment with them there on account of My people, My heritage Israel, whom they have scattered among the nations; they have also divided up My land."*　　　verses 1–2

God is going to judge the nations on the basis of how they have treated the Jewish people. Particularly, He is going to judge them for one error: they have divided up His land.

The modern political word for dividing up the land is *partition.* This is precisely what the nations have done and are busy trying to do right now—and God is angry with them. We who love our nation need to be in urgent prayer that our nation will not be aligned against God's purposes for Israel.

Joel does not say if there will be any Jews judged at this time. My personal opinion is that the Jews will have already passed through their own judgment, the Great Tribulation. Somebody said years ago something worth considering: "God blesses the Jews direct; He blesses the Gentiles through the Jews. God judges the Gentiles direct; He judges the Jews through the Gentiles." I believe this has been worked out in history time and time again.

Israel will pass through their judgment in the Great Tribulation. They will have been judged, but then the nations that persecuted them will be judged. In Matthew 25 Jesus reiterates this. It is clear to me that this is a recounting of Joel 3 in the New Testament.

> *When the Son of Man comes in His glory, and all the holy angels with Him, then He will sit on the throne of His glory.* [This is the same scene as in Joel 3:1.] *All the nations* [the Gentiles] *will be gathered before Him, and He will separate them one from another, as a shepherd divides his sheep from the goats.*
> 　　　　　　　　　　　　　　　*Matthew 25:31–32*

If you study Matthew 25, you will find that the basis of the division of the sheep from the goats is how they have treated the brothers of Jesus—the Jewish people. We need to speak out and warn our nation, "You're going to be judged by the way you have dealt with God's people and God's land, Israel." (We will study this judgment in greater detail in a subsequent study on eternal judgment.)

Establishment of Christ's millennial kingdom

Following the judgment of the nations, Christ's kingdom on earth will be established. Whenever Christians pray the Lord's Prayer, which they probably do quite often, what they may not realize is they are praying for the establishment of Christ's kingdom on earth.

The first petition is "Thy kingdom come" (Matthew 6:10 KJV). That takes precedence over all other petitions. When we are praying that, we are actually praying for the return of Jesus and the establishment of His kingdom on the earth, whether we are aware of it or not.

The establishment of His kingdom is described in Isaiah 24 and is, in a sense, a description of the climax of the age. This scene is duplicated many times in Revelation:

> *The earth is violently broken, the earth is split open, the earth is shaken exceedingly. The earth shall reel to and fro like a drunkard, and shall totter like a hut; its transgression shall be heavy upon it, and it will fall, and not rise again.* [That is Earth, the planet on which we live.] *It shall come to pass in that day that the LORD will punish on high the host of exalted ones, and on the earth the kings of the earth.*   Isaiah 24:19–21

The Lord will deal with two kingdoms: Satan's kingdom in the heavenlies and the kingdom of man on earth. He will punish all those who refuse His righteous government in the person of Jesus.

They will be gathered together, as prisoners are gathered
in the pit [or prison], *and will be shut up in the prison;*
after many days they will be punished. [And this is the
climax:] *Then the moon will be disgraced and the sun*
ashamed; for the LORD *of hosts will reign on Mount Zion*
and in Jerusalem and before His elders, gloriously.
verses 22–23

The Lord's kingdom will have been reestablished in its capital,
which is Jerusalem. Why should the sun be ashamed and the moon
disgraced? I believe the answer is in Luke in the description of
the return of Jesus. Jesus said:

"For whoever is ashamed of Me and My words, of him the
Son of Man will be ashamed when He comes in His own
glory, and in His Father's [glory], *and* [the glory] *of the*
holy angels."   *Luke 9:26*

Jesus is coming in His own glory, the glory of the Father
and the glory of the holy angels. The brilliance of that glory is
something that we cannot even begin to imagine, and yet it will
not hurt our eyes. His glory will be such that the sun and the
moon will have to take a back seat, because the light they offer is
nothing compared with the glory that comes with Jesus. That is
why they will be ashamed.

It is at this time that Jesus will establish His kingdom for a
thousand years. "A thousand years," the Bible says, "[is] as one
day" (2 Peter 3:8). It is just one day in the Lord's reckoning.

This period is called the Millennium from the Latin words for
"thousand," *mille*, and for "year," *annum*. We know it will be a
thousand years because Revelation 20:4–6 tells us that the saints
who were martyred during the Great Tribulation will be resurrected
at this time and "they shall be priests of God and of Christ, and
shall reign with Him a thousand years" (verse 6).

Christ's millennial kingdom will be a time unlike any other
in human history. It is the subject of numerous Old Testament
prophecies such as Isaiah 11:6–10; 65:17–25 and Malachi 4:3–5.

Revelation 20 also tells us that during this thousand year period of time Satan and his demons will be bound up and unable to deceive the nations.

He laid hold of the dragon, that serpent of old, who is the Devil and Satan, and bound him for a thousand years; and he cast him into the bottomless pit, and shut him up, and set a seal on him, so that he should deceive the nations no more till the thousand years were finished. But after these things he must be released for a little while.

Revelation 20:2–3

Without the continual intervention of evil in the earth, it will be a time without warfare and fear; a period of great prosperity and abundance and a time when disease and sickness will have been eliminated or greatly reduced.

Can you imagine what the world will be like? This is the hope that mankind has tried to achieve through political philosophies and technology throughout history. It will only come about, however, when Jesus returns. It can never be achieved by human effort.

Satan briefly released from his prison at the end of the Millennium

John describes Satan's last attempt to oppose the authority of God and of Christ and to stir up rebellion against that authority. This occurs at the end of the Millennium.

Now when the thousand years have expired, Satan will be released from his prison and will go out to deceive the nations which are in the four corners of the earth, Gog and Magog, to gather them together to battle, whose number is as the sand of the sea. They went up on the breadth of the earth and surrounded the camp of the saints and the beloved city. And fire came down from God out of heaven and devoured them. And the devil, who deceived them, was cast into the lake of fire and brimstone where the beast and the false prophet are. And they will be tormented day and night forever and ever. Revelation 20:7–10

John uses the phrases "the camp of the saints" and "the beloved city" to describe the city of Jerusalem and the territory surrounding that city. During the Millennium, Jerusalem will be the earthly center of Christ's administration and rule over the nations of the earth.

Satan will be released by God to go out and stir up rebellion in the nations once again. This is one of his jobs. He is used by God to manifest what is in the hearts of men. Because of the presence of Christ on the earth during the Millennium, evil will lie dormant in men's hearts. But when Satan is loosed, he will stir up the nations to one final rebellion against God (Revelation 20:8–9).

However, the Lord will intervene and bring final judgment on the nations. Then Satan will be thrown into the lake of fire together with the Antichrist and the false prophet, who are already there.

The present heaven and the present earth pass away; a new heaven and a new earth come forth

The psalmist says of the creation:

Of old You laid the foundation of the earth, and the heavens are the work of Your hands. They will perish, but You will endure; yes, they will all grow old like a garment; like a cloak You will change them, and they will be changed.
Psalm 102:25–26

At the end of time, this physical creation will have accomplished the purpose for which God created it. He will create a new one "in which righteousness dwells" (2 Peter 3:13). The most amazing statement of all is in Revelation 21:5:

Then He who sat on the throne said, "Behold, I make all things new." [Nothing of the old is going to persist. It's all going to be done away with.] *And He said to me, "Write, for these words are true and faithful."*

It seems to me that John could not really believe that all this was going to happen. So the Lord said to him, "Put it down. It's all true. It's all going to happen. I'm going to make all things new. There will be no corruption left. No taint of sin. No stains. Not even any guilty consciences." That is God's program—as high above our program as heaven is above earth.

And I saw a new heaven and a new earth, for the first heaven and the first earth had passed away. Also there was no more sea. And I, John, saw the holy city, New Jerusalem, coming down out of heaven from God, prepared as a bride adorned for her husband. And I heard a loud voice from heaven saying, "Behold, the tabernacle of God is with men, and He will dwell with them, and they shall be His people, and God Himself will be with them and be their God. And God will wipe away every tear from their eyes; there shall be no more death, nor sorrow, nor crying; and there shall be no more pain, for the former things have passed away." Revelation 21:1–5

This is a picture of total redemption from vanity in every form. Travail, sorrow, birth pains, sickness, disease—all are wiped out.

Verse 9 continues, "Come, I will show you the bride, the Lamb's wife." The angel then showed John the New Jerusalem. Remember, the New Jerusalem is not heaven. It is the final manifestation of the Body of Christ on earth. This is His supreme purpose: to find in us a dwelling place in which He can thereafter make Himself available to all creation.

Resurrection and judgment of all remaining dead

There will be one final judgment for mankind. All those who were not previously judged by the Lord will be resurrected and will stand before a great white throne. This is not just a magistrate's seat of judgment, but a king's throne. The time will not be at the beginning of the millennial kingdom, but at its close.

The judgment of believers is before the judgment seat of Christ before the millennial kingdom. The judgment of unbelievers is before a great white throne at the close of the millennial kingdom.

The judgment of unbelievers, those who were not resurrected in the resurrection of the righteous, is found in Revelation 20:11–15. John paints a most awesome and vivid picture of what this final and great judgment will be like:

Then I saw a great white throne and Him who sat on it, from whose face the earth and heaven fled away. And there was found no place for them. And I saw the dead, small and great, standing before God, and books were opened. And another book was opened, which is the Book of Life. And the dead were judged according to their works, by the things which were written in the books. The sea gave up the dead who were in it, and Death and Hades [Sheol, the place of departed spirits] *delivered up the dead who were in them. And they were judged, each one according to his works. Then Death and Hades were cast into the lake of fire. This is the second death* [the irrevocable, eternal banishment from the presence of Almighty God, but not a cessation of consciousness. Once we become beings, consciousness continues forever and ever.] *And anyone not found written in the Book of Life was cast into the lake of fire.*

First, these people are called "the dead." John says, "I saw the dead, small and great, standing before God." Even after resurrection and their bodies had been restored to them, they were still dead. Dead in trespasses and sins; alienated and cut off from the life of God; resurrected in their bodies to receive judgment for what they had done in their bodies.

Second, the books were opened. These are universal records kept of everything that everyone has ever done. This speaks of universal accountability. Every one of us will be required to answer for what we have done. Man is accountable to his Creator, who will one day be his Judge.

At this final moment in history, nothing else will be of any consequence—not how famous, wealthy, or popular anyone might have been. The only thing that will matter is whether or not their name is written in the Book of Life, because that will determine whether they spend eternity in God's presence or in the lake of fire with Satan and his angels. (This judgment will be considered in detail in our study of the foundational doctrine, *Eternal Judgment*.)

Jesus hands over the kingdom to the Father

At this point, Jesus has completely accomplished His work. He has put all the enemies of God under subjection and abolished the last great enemy—death itself. Now that Jesus is the unchallenged Lord of all things, He delivers the kingdom up to His Father.

> *Then comes the end, when He delivers the kingdom to God the Father, when He puts an end to all rule and all authority and power. For He* [Christ] *must reign till He* [the Father] *has put all enemies under His feet. . . . Now when all things are made subject to Him* [Christ], *then the Son Himself will also be subject to Him* [the Father], *who put all things under Him, that God may be all in all.*
> *1 Corinthians 15:24–25, 28*

This final phase of the establishment of God's kingdom is called "the dispensation of the fullness of the times" (Ephesians 1:10). It represents the complete and final establishment of God's order and government in the universe. We have a special place in this dispensation because we first trusted in Christ. Throughout all ages, we shall be to the praise of the glory of His grace.

This is a marvelous picture of the heart of Jesus, because He never sought a kingdom for His own sake. Everything He did was motivated by a single passion: His love for His Father. This should be a great challenge to all of us in everything we do. Are we doing it for ourselves, or for the Father?

It would be fitting, if you are so moved, to pray this prayer in response to this message:

> *Father, help me to train my eyes to see the eternal, invisible realm rather than the temporary, visible aspects of my life.*

Help me to remember that this earth is not my eternal home.

Let me not despise prophecy, but look forward with expectation to the soon coming of my Lord and Savior, Jesus Christ. Help me to discern end-time events in light of biblical prophecy—that I might be ready to meet the Lord Jesus when He comes. Amen.

• • • •

Get the Complete Laying the Foundations Series

1. Founded on the Rock (B100)

2. Authority and Power of God's Word (B101)

3. Through Repentance to Faith (B102)

4. Faith and Works (B103)

5. The Doctrine of Baptisms (B104)

6. Immersion in The Spirit (B105)

7. Transmitting God's Power (B106)

8. At the End of Time (B107)

9. Resurrection of the Body (B108)

10. Final Judgment (B109)

www.derekprince.com

About the Author

Derek Prince (1915–2003) was born in India of British parents. Educated as a scholar of Greek and Latin at Eton College and Cambridge University, England, he held a Fellowship in Ancient and Modern Philosophy at King's College. He also studied several modern languages, including Hebrew and Aramaic, at Cambridge University and the Hebrew University in Jerusalem.

While serving with the British army in World War II, he began to study the Bible and experienced a life-changing encounter with Jesus Christ. Out of this encounter he formed two conclusions: first, that Jesus Christ is alive; second, that the Bible is a true, relevant, up-to-date book. These conclusions altered the whole course of his life, which he then devoted to studying and teaching the Bible.

Derek's main gift of explaining the Bible and its teaching in a clear and simple way has helped build a foundation of faith in millions of lives. His non-denominational, non-sectarian approach has made his teaching equally relevant and helpful to people from all racial and religious backgrounds.

He is the author of over 50 books, 600 audio and 100 video teachings, many of which have been translated and published in more than 100 languages. His daily radio broadcast is translated into Arabic, Chinese (Amoy, Cantonese, Mandarin, Shanghaiese, Swatow), Croatian, German, Malagasy, Mongolian, Russian, Samoan, Spanish and Tongan. The radio program continues to touch lives around the world.

Derek Prince Ministries persists in reaching out to believers in over 140 countries with Derek's teachings, fulfilling the mandate to keep on "until Jesus returns." This is effected through the outreaches of more than 45 Derek Prince offices around the world, including primary work in Australia, Canada, China, France, Germany, the Netherlands, New Zealand, Norway, Russia, South Africa, Switzerland, the United Kingdom and the United States. For current information about these and other worldwide locations, visit www.derekprince.com.

Derek Prince Ministries
Offices Worldwide

ASIA/ PACIFIC
DPM–Asia/Pacific
38 Hawdon Street, Sydenham
Christchurch 8023,
New Zealand
T: + 64 3 366 4443
E: admin@dpm.co.nz
W: www.dpm.co.nz and
www.derekprince.in

AUSTRALIA
DPM–Australia
1st Floor, 134 Pendle Way
Pendle Hill
New South Wales 2145, Australia
T: + 612 9688 4488
E: enquiries@derekprince.com.au
W: www.derekprince.com.au

CANADA
DPM–Canada
P. O. Box 8354 Halifax,
Nova Scotia B3K 5M1, Canada
T: + 1 902 443 9577
E: enquiries.dpm@eastlink.ca
W: www.derekprince.org

FRANCE
DPM–France
B.P. 31, Route d'Oupia,
34210 Olonzac,
France
T: + 33 468 913872
E: info@derekprince.fr
W: www.derekprince.fr

GERMANY
DPM–Germany
Schwarzauer Str. 56
D-83308 Trostberg,
Germany
T: + 49 8621 64146
E: IBL.de@t-online.de
W: www.ibl-dpm.net

NETHERLANDS
DPM–Netherlands
P. O. Box 349
1960 AH Heemskerk,
The Netherlands
T: + 31 251 255 044
E: info@nl.derekprince.com
W: www.dpmnederland.nl

NORWAY
P. O. Box 129 Lodderfjord
N-5881, Bergen,
Norway
T: +47 928 39855
E: sverre@derekprince.no
W: www.derekprince.no

SINGAPORE
Derek Prince
Publications Pte. Ltd.
P. O. Box 2046 ,
Robinson Road Post Office
Singapore 904046
T: + 65 6392 1812
E: dpmchina@singnet.com.sg
English web: www.dpmchina.org
Chinese web: www.ygmweb.org

Lightning Source UK Ltd.
Milton Keynes UK
UKOW030934310512

193692UK00001B/8/P